Untangling the World

Vinita Rawani

BookLeaf Publishing

India | USA | UK

Presentation by *BookLeaf Publishing*

Web: www.bookleafpub.com

E-mail: info@bookleafpub.com

ISBN: 9789358315288

First edition 2024

ACKNOWLEDGEMENT

I am so grateful for the people in my life who have given me so much strength and courage. They have fostered a safe haven where I could authentically embrace who I am, encouraging me to be bold and chart my own path. Through their guidance, I've learned the art of loving—accepting it, nurturing it in the smallest moments, cherishing it within friendships, and most importantly, within myself. Each person I've encountered has played a role in deepening my understanding and appreciation for myself. I also want to show my gratitude to my sister Anisha for helping me design the book cover and for always being here for me.

PREFACE

Whenever I feel an emotion or thought strongly, the poems seem to start writing themselves. My feelings get poured onto the pages, making me see the silver lining, the beauty of what I have created. It's always easy to write these poems but harder if I have to read them twice. The thought of sharing these poems makes me uneasy but with every passing moment, I also feel a sense of courage.

Hiding behind the pages

It was always easier to hide in these pages,
Where the ink told my stories,
So permanent yet so beautifully written.
The only place safe enough to shallow my
secrets.

I couldn't be disappointed by these still pages,
Instead they granted me the freedom,
The space to be myself,
Without any judgment,
Without any fear,
Without any pressures.
The only true place where I could be vulnerable.

So I wrote pages and pages of thoughts,
The one that I was never going to share.
It wasn't just a diary of secrets,
But a piece of myself.

That was a young girl so afraid,
Afraid of not knowing who she was,
Afraid of finding out who she was,
How her tears carried the depth of the ocean.
How her smile carried the hope of the future.

I have never trusted fate,
To write my story.
Too often the writers of my story have been
other people,
Too often I didn't like how it goes.
Never my choice, never about my happiness,
But now I will be selfish.

I will write my own story,
I will share my stories.
I will give the power to myself.

Stay?

I came from a whole different world,
Dropped into an unknown place,
With no strings to people or the culture.
A few months of turmoil,
Wanting to go back,
Because how could I stay?
Where no one looked at me as their own.
Slow and steady wins the race, doesn't it.
Different clothes, different food.
New accent, a new me.
Now how couldn't I stay?
When the mask had became real.

Belonging

I live here, I breathe the same air as them,
But somehow I don't feel like I belong.
No matter how much I change,
How hard I try to be like them.
I can't really change who I am or
Where I come from.
Most importantly, where I come from.
I love my roots,
It makes me feel special and proud.
But my roots make me different,
Which means it's not allowed to exist.
At least not in the open but just in the shadows.
So I have to live with it, not others
Because others want it comfortable.
I can't forget who I am or what makes me
different,
Just like they can't.

Curse or a Blessing

It's like they are both speaking different
languages,
It's like the tug of war and you don't know
which side is yours,
It's like the rainbow that comes after the rain,
It's the silver linings.

Isn't this the perfect American dream or rather
the beautiful British dream?
Why wouldn't it be?

I always loved fairy tales a bit too much,
I think I knew they were too good to be true,
But they would take you to a world of hope.
I liked being in that world.
Hiding away from the pain.
Believing that someone could save me if I really
was lost.

I was lost in a far away strange land,
Where no one looked liked me,
Thought like me,
Ate like me.
It was almost a dream,
Where nothing made sense.

I kept on wondering when I will wake up,
Wake up in my own home.

Strangers became friends,
Friends who didn't need to be taught to be kind.
Even if they didn't understand, it didn't matter.
My accent didn't match theirs,
It was okay.
I didn't understand their jokes,
It was okay.
I didn't know who I was,
It was okay.

Even if someone can't understand you,
Their presence might just be enough,
Powerful enough.
Those friends who were once strangers were
now family.

What was once a land of a language my mum
could barely speak,
Now became this girl's home filled with dreams.

Sometimes I still dream of my old home,
Wondering what could have been if I never left.

Who did I want to be?

It never occurred to me to notice people's eye
colours,
Or their hair colours.
It was almost always the same.
Until it wasn't.

Then my beautiful long black hair didn't seem as
exciting.
I wanted to see how those brown highlights
would look on me.
I would envy how easily they could dye their
hair,
They could be anything they wanted to be.

While I always couldn't have that freedom.
I was so different to them,
So comparing myself was instincts at this point.

The culture that was so rich and beautiful,
Was slowly becoming the restrains that I just
wanted to escape.

The rules that I followed wasn't made for this
new world,
So I would envy them.

Because they didn't have these rules to make
them feel guilty,
To make them question everything,
To make them jealous of what they didn't have.

So I abandoned parts of my culture at places
unknown,
It's been years and I feel their absence in those
still moments,
How I yearn those lost parts of myself,
My identity, my childhood and a place that I
used to call home.

Who was I and where I belonged is a question I
don't know if I can ever answer.
I wanted to and needed to fit into the society's
mould,
So I could feel like I belonged.
So I could stop being an outsider.

It didn't matter what I did, where I was,
It didn't stop me from feeling out of place.
It wasn't until I had met people who were kind.
People who accepted me for who I am,
People who loved me, who saw me beyond my
cultural identity.
I didn't have to try to be Indian or try to be
British, I could be myself,

Because my culture isn't the only thing that
defines me.

How I look speaks loudly as I enter any room,
Who I am is defined solely by my culture too
often,
My culture is a part of me,
Not something that can consume my whole
being.
I try to see who I am when people already know
who they think I am.
When people have already decided who I am,
I have to try,
To be fearless and choose who I am and who I
want to become.

Beautiful Dreams

When you are the eldest daughter,
You get to be everything,
You get to try every role that exists,
If that's being your mum's caretaker,
Or being your dad's son,
Or being a mediator between your sisters.

What you don't always get to be is yourself,
Sometimes you wonder,
If who you are is really you,
Or the fragments of your family,
If you are their dreams, their do-over,
A lesson from their regrets,
Or a chance at happiness.

All those beautiful dreams sometimes hang over
you like anchors that were never meant to pull
you down.
They were supposed to lift you up in a hot air
balloon filled of hope.

Sometimes I would rather cycle on the ground
through the hills,
Just so I could watch the sunset.

Memories

So many people come and visit your door step,
Some come inside your house,
Some stay forever,
Some leave,
Some never find the path to your door.

Isn't it amazing all the people who find the path
to your door?
Each decorate your house with a fragment of
themselves,
So you can always remember them,
In the joy, in the tears, in the quiet, in the chaos.

And how we always remember them, in the most
unexpected of times,
Unexpected places,
Unexpected people.

How a memory,
Something we can't touch,
But only feel,
Feels so heavy.
I guess it carries a piece of your heart.
I guess it holds on tightly before time loosens its
grips.

A memory, a moment that shouldn't change
shape, colour or size.
Changes so easily with every passing moment.
It's not a painting of a moment,
Instead it becomes a reflection of the present
moment,
A reflection of what you feel.
It takes the shape of what you feel,
If that is gratitude, anger, sadness or joy.
So can memories really be trusted,
Or should we instead listen to what we truly feel
in that moment of reminiscence?

The twinkling stars

A sky empty of twinkling stars, she doesn't
even notice,
I wish she could see the magic of a falling star
so she could make a wish,
But she would say, it's okay didi, I have a
dandelion.
I would smile and remember, maybe the magic
wasn't in the stars but how my grandpa would
tell me stories.

Nostalgia

It's incredible how different places remind you
of home,
How different people's smiles and jokes remind
you of someone you know,
Is it that you carry pieces of home and people
wherever you go?

Is it that you find a connection in places
unknown?
To seek the comfort somewhere you don't know?

Is it because you remember the beautiful places
and memories,
And don't want to forget them somewhere new?

There's a comfort in memories that don't change
as you change,
You can hold on to them forever,
Because that's the good thing about the past, it
can never change.
They remind you of a time that's worth having
hope for,
People leave this imprint on you of hope and
strength and they are the ones you never forget.

So can you create a new home without
decorating it first with fragments of places you
have been and people you have met?

Sunflower

You are a petal of my sunflower,
The one who attracts the sunshine of happiness
for me.
But when the sun gets lost in the dark clouds,
And it can't send us it's rays of hope.
Then we turn to each other,
Just like sunflowers do.
Because no matter where we are, if it's a
twinkling night or a sky full of tears, we will
always have each other.

It's funny how people find each other,
Just a random combination of coincidences.
We end up being exactly where we are supposed
to be,
without looking,
We find the reason for our happy existence.

I don't know what made us click,
If it was the killer bee, or the cute but scary dog,
Or bonding over the hot Thor.
Think the animals were trying their best to make
us friends.
Just like they do in fairytales.

The hot chocolate and your cute smile definitely
sweetened the deal.

Second year was the year of tests and exams and
assessments,
Not the academic ones but our friendship ones.
We must have passed every single friendship test
in the hurricane of obstacles we faced.
As strong as the wind was trying to pull us away,
and the dirt in our eyes, making it hard to see
what we have.
Our friendship didn't crumble into pieces,
It only bloomed like the beautiful periwinkles.

What the characters in the screen taught me

I found warmth in the stories on the tv,
Found friends in the characters on the screen.
Felt their sorrow as they were mine,
Felt their joy like I was in their world.

It was an escape, it was a remedy, it was another world,
That I wished to be in.
They always promised to have a happy ending.
How I so desperately wanted to know if I would
have that happy ending too.
They gave me hope, gave me inspiration, gave me
me role models.

I learned to be kind, to be brave, to be honest
just like how they were,
I learned to believe that anything was possible,
That it was all meant to be,
It was fate, not just merely coincidences.
It was the magic, that wasn't in my world.
It was a saviour, that wasn't in my world.
It was the definite happy ending, that wasn't in
my world.

I felt so deeply,
That I could shed tears for the ones on the
screen,
I felt a part of their world,
How their tragedy could ruin my days,
How their miracle could create a world of hope.
They taught me to be brave, to be good, and to
love freely.
That good people receive their happy endings,
That everything will be okay in the end.
They taught me more about life than the books
from the school ever did.

World that I live in

I live in a world with so much chaos,
With so much discomfort and pain.
Someone else might have given that to me but
now it's mine to own.
My thoughts continue to live in the pain,
It finds comfort in the discomfort,
Because that's what I know.
Years of being broken, now I know how to surf
the waves of sadness.
I know how to survive.
So I like staying in my old pain, a place I have
already conquered instead of,
Being somewhere new and unknown,
Where I don't have a sword in my hand,
And a shield as chest to protect me.
I don't know if that's wrong,
But I have been through too much to leave the
home I know.
There are a few who have shown me the path to
leave and I am collecting the courage slowly to
walk those footsteps.
I heal with every footstep, I heal with every
person.

The word 'love'

We complain that some words have two
meanings but why do we forget the words like
love?
The confusion, the dread and the hope it brings.

Love surprises you.
It's never what you expect it to be.
It's everything and nothing like the movies.

It holds so much power,
In seconds it can turn hate to nothing,
In seconds it can make you forget the reason for
your existence.

It's also the illusion that you can only find the
romantic kind of love,
But love exists in every corner of the world,
Every moment in your day.
It's in the laugh with your sisters,
It's in the secrets that you share with your
friends,
It's in the praise you get from dad,
It's in the way your mum never stops taking care
of you,
Or in the wisdom your grandparents share.

Maybe that love is not the one which makes
your heart beat fast,
But it's the one which gives you the strength to
live,
Gives you the pen to write your dreams with and
the fuel to ignite your passion with.

I guess love means different things to people,
Something that can be found in different people
for each person.
I think we will always want the kind of love that
we don't have.

Learning to love myself

I don't know if I could ever learn how to love
myself all on my own,
I was never taught to,
I was never showed how to.
I didn't know what love was.
What unconditional love was.

Love was always a reward,
An accomplishment, an achievement,
If I had done something right,
If I hadn't done anything wrong.
So I learned to be perfect,
To receive all that love.

How unfamiliar was the concept of
unconditional love,
A love without expectations, without
responsibilities, without duties.
A love that I never knew.

Sometimes the way you love yourself is a
reflection,
Reflection of how others love you.
How others teach you to love,
Because how can you know any better.

It wasn't until I was shown that I could be loved,
Without having to give anything back,
Without having to be anything except myself.
How love could stay,
Even with my mistakes,
Even with my failures,
Even with my imperfections.

I don't think I could have learned how to love
myself,
If people hadn't shown me how.
People come and touch your soul,
Leaving the greatest gift that one could be left
with,
Finally knowing how to love myself without any
expectations.

Secrets of the Universe

We know the secrets of the Universe.
Why light exists?
Why the moon shines so bright?
How the stars can tell you everything.

Still we don't understand ourselves or others.
We are such complicated beings.
Having to live with the existential problem of
knowing who we are.
Knowing what we want.
Knowing where we want to go.

Knowing someone, understanding someone is a
quest in it's self.
Knowing someone is like peeling the layers of
an onion,
The more layers that go, the more tears you
shed.
Because you understand the weight that they
carry in their heart,
The burden they carry in their shoulders,
What makes them who they are today.
Which tells you the story behind their choices.
What makes them laugh, What makes them cry.

I think love is understanding someone,
As being loved is to be understood.

So I think in order to love yourself,
You also have to understand yourself.
You have to create that safety, that comfort, that
care so you can simply be yourself.
Then observe all the appreciation you will
receive from yourself,
Maybe even forgiveness.

The fortress built brick by brick

I think we confuse,
What is supposed to be easy,
What is supposed to be simple.

All my life I have learned,
To be hard working, passionate and committed,
Thinking the world only meant it for my studies.
Then it took me the absence of it to see the
presence of it all around me.

Look closely and you will see it in your
friendships, your family, your love,
In what you would do for yourself.
This isn't supposed to be easy or simple,
We have to work hard, be loving and be
consistent to make it easy and simple.
It's not luck, fate or it being right,
It's our actions.
If you neglect it, It will be too complicated to
untangle.
If you give up, if you stop trying,
Then you lose pieces of yourself or of people
that you might never find.

Trust, care and love is what makes it easy,
Makes it simple.
It's a fortress that can't be built in one day,
It's brick by brick of tears, of smiles, of the
shared moments of not giving up.
It's first staying when it's not easy or simple.
That's why some relations, friendships can last
so long,
It's people choosing to love, to care, to not give
up.
It's two people helping each other build that
fortress together slowly,
So they can take shelter there together when it's
dark and stormy outside.

It's not a race

Sometimes I am so harsh on myself,
To be perfect,
To be productive all the time,
To have done everything in my life,
It's like this race to win, to have everything.
And then it hits me I am only 20.

I don't need to be this finished piece of work,
I don't need to know what I want,
Where I want to go.

To solve all my life's problems with a good
routine, healthy diet and good marks.

Instead I am a working piece of art,
Beautifully built from the wisdom gained from
mistakes,
Still waiting to experience all the colours of life.
Still waiting to meet all the different artists who
will leave an imprint.

How can we forget that art isn't perfection,
It's a symbol of hard work, passion and
commitment.
It's different colours fusing together,
One might even call it a mess,

Its's a combination of strokes that come together
perfectly to create beauty.

Your beauty might not be understood by
everyone,
Doesn't mean it's not worth appreciating.
Just because you are not a finished piece of
work,
Doesn't mean it's not worth admiring.

Art takes time, we take time, we have to be
patient with ourselves.
We can't expect ourselves to know everything,
be everything this young.
It's not about getting it all right,
It's definitely not about waiting until it's perfect
to be happy, to live, to enjoy.

It's not a race,
Atleast it shouldn't be,
It's a walk,
It has uphills, downhills and some fog,
But you don't have to see the destination,
You just have to observe the beauty,
Admire it, embrace it, fall in love with it.
Share the journey,
Fill your jar with the memories.
And even if you are lost,
Just keep walking.

Girl and her keys

I am a girl,
Made up of thousands of boxes,
All requiring a key that I so preciously hold.
Never giving too many keys to the same person,
Never sharing all my keys.

It's easier,
It's safer to share one key with one person,
Because god forbid it if they know me
completely.

It's easier,
It's safer to trust each person a little bit with
your secrets,
Then to trust one person completely.
Because if I have more keys then the person
standing in front of me,
Then I still have power.

Each key unlocks who I am,
Helps you understand me.
And easily gives you the chance to judge me.

I usually do give out the keys too often,
It's in my nature.

Or maybe I need to know, I need to confirm.
Because trusting them when there is nothing to
lose is easier.
I guess the thought of sharing the burden of the
keys is too tempting.
If I could give out all my keys,
Then the heaviness wouldn't hold me down,
And I wouldn't be the girl with all the locked
boxes.

The way that I am

I am not dumb for caring,
That's just who I am.
I am a mirror,
That's how I was made.
I reflect the tears, I reflect the smiles.
If I didn't, how would I understand.
Understand the pain,
Understand the beauty of who you are.
How would I show my love?
If I didn't feel what you felt.

I can never stop trying,
I can never give up on people.
If I cared about you,
I always will.
It's a promise to myself.
Just because I saw the glimmer of light inside
you.
It's not up to me though,
If you choose to make me brighter with that light
or if you choose to burn me.
I am fearless,
I never think about being burned,
I always jump for that hope.

Maybe because I need that light to see what's
inside me.

I need to care, I need to love, I need to be kind.
Or the world wouldn't make sense to me.
Who would I be without it,
What would I do,
What would be my purpose?
I guess I was never taught to live for myself.
Or I live in the endless hope,
That if I care, if I love, if I show kindness,
Then maybe there won't be room for pain in
what I receive.

I don't like losing things,
Maybe that's why I never give up.
Once I have it, once I care about it,
Then how can I ever give it up.
Or maybe because I have lost so much of myself
over the years,
That now I just want to hold on to everything
dear.

Parts of myself

I always had to be perfect,
Be exactly what the other person needed me to
be.
A listener, a talker, just not myself.
If I was perfect, if I was needed,
Then they would never have a reason to leave.
I hated being left,
The idea that someone couldn't find a reason to
stay.

Was I not worth staying for?
I could tell you all the reasons to stay,
How I am so beautiful, so smart, so kind,
I knew I was worth everything.

Maybe the someone who needed to stay was me,
The someone who should never leave myself is
me.

I could talk your ears off if I felt a sense of
safety,
If I felt like I could finally be myself without
apology,
If someone cared enough to listen.

But if I feel even a hint of threat, I would go
back in my shell like a turtle,
Be as quiet and still like the night.
If you can't hear me, if I am invisible then you
can't hurt me.

It's not easy to try and understand myself,
Because I see parts that aren't strong,
Or beautiful,
The parts that I wish I didn't have,
Because I picked up these parts in places of fear.
I see now that every part is worth it because it's
a piece of myself.
So I will stay,
I will,
because I am worth everything.

Sharing these poems

Sharing these poems,
Is sharing stories from the corners of my heart,
That I hid away,
In fear of people finding out who I really am.
I don't know if that's scared, hurt or broken.
Or if that's just a girl wanting to be happy.

It's terrifying,
Having these written in a book,
When I had never shared a single thought with
the people I love.
It's like opening a door to my mind,
Giving people a chance to understand me.
I have never trusted anyone to understand me.
Maybe because I could never understand myself.

I feel like someone will reveal who I am,
Or maybe just simply ask me If I am okay.
If people don't know what's going on,
Then I can pretend to be strong,
For others,
For myself.
I can pretend.
If they find out,
Can I still be strong?

I have always kept myself hidden,
Never showing what I truly feel.
Never reacting how I really want.
Never crying in front of someone,
Just incase they hurt me.

Writing this book is giving the key away,
Finally letting everything I have been holding so
tight,
And close to my chest go.
It could be a mistake,
It could become regret,
Or it could be the perfect way to give power to
myself.